Piano Pronto

Christmas Solos
for Late Beginners

Music by
Jennifer Eklund

PIANO PRONTO PUBLISHING

PianoPronto.com

Christmas Solos for Late Beginners

Jennifer Eklund

Copyright ©2015 by Piano Pronto Publishing, Inc. (ASCAP)
All Rights Reserved.

WARNING: The compositions, arrangements, text, and graphics in this publication are protected by copyright law. No part of this work may be duplicated or reprinted without the prior consent of the author.

ISBN 978-0-9899084-3-6

Piano Pronto Publishing
PianoPronto.com

Christmas Solos
for Late Beginners

TABLE OF CONTENTS

AWAY IN A MANGER 1

DING DONG! MERRILY ON HIGH 2

DECK THE HALLS. 3

HERE WE COME A-CAROLING 5

JINGLE BELLS 7

JOY TO THE WORLD. 9

SILENT NIGHT 11

THE FIRST NOEL 13

WE THREE KINGS. 15

UKRAINIAN BELL CAROL 17

WE WISH YOU A MERRY CHRISTMAS. 19

O HOLY NIGHT 21

O COME, O COME, EMMANUEL 23

THE TWELVE DAYS OF CHRISTMAS 25

Music by
Jennifer Eklund

PianoPronto.com

1. Away in a Manger

Traditional
Arr. Jennifer Eklund

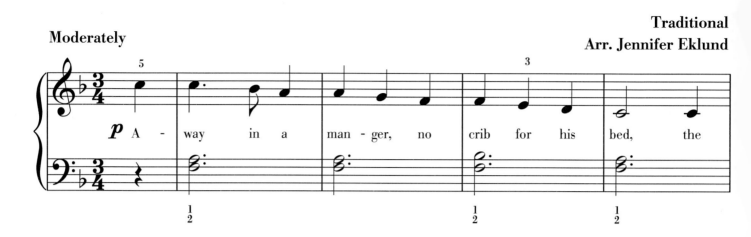
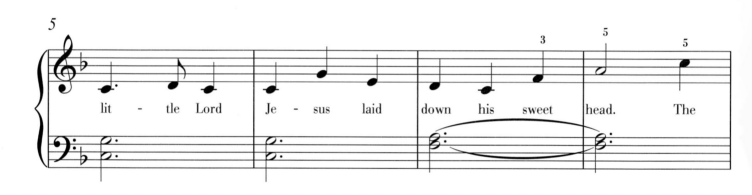
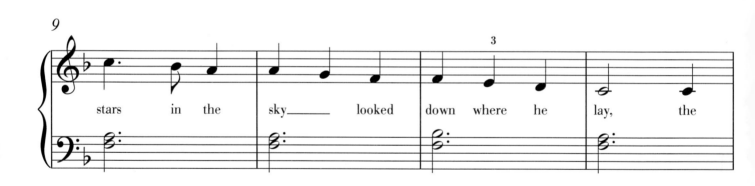

2. Ding Dong! Merrily on High

Traditional
Arr. Jennifer Eklund

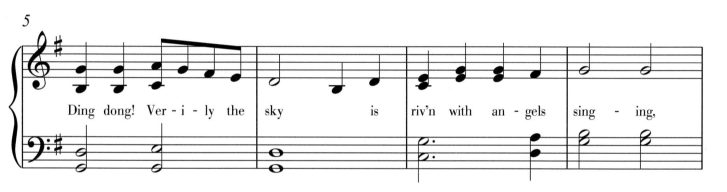

Copyright © 2015 Piano Pronto Publishing, Inc. (ASCAP)
All Rights Reserved | PianoPronto.com

3. Deck the Halls

Traditional
Arr. Jennifer Eklund

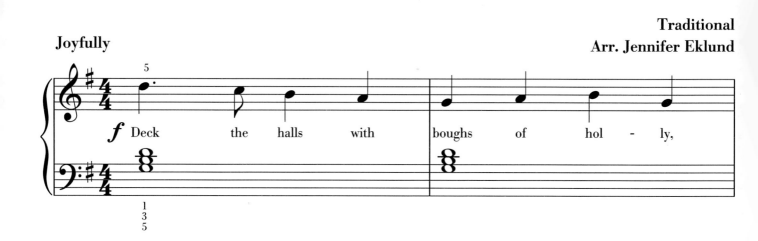
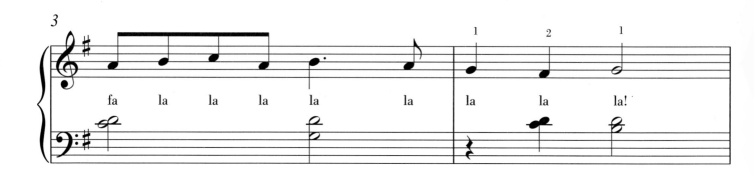
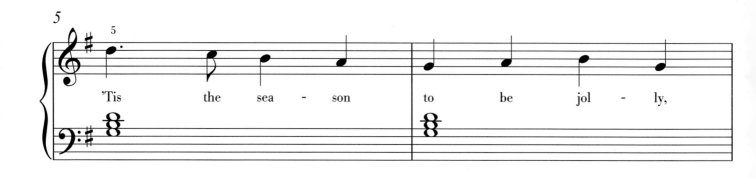

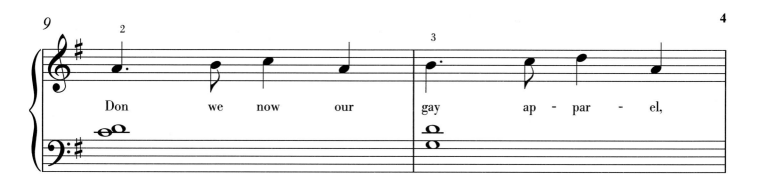
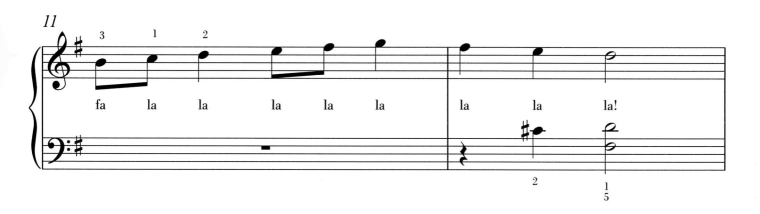
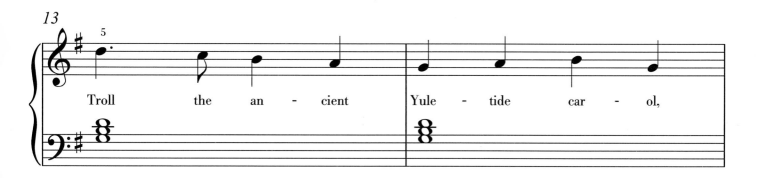

4. Here We Come A-Caroling

Traditional
Arr. Jennifer Eklund

Quickly in 1

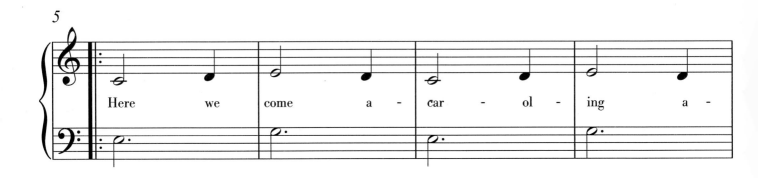
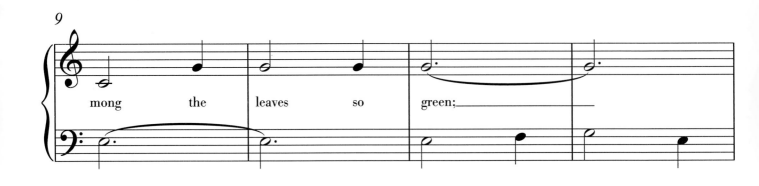

Copyright © 2015 Piano Pronto Publishing, Inc. (ASCAP)
All Rights Reserved | PianoPronto.com

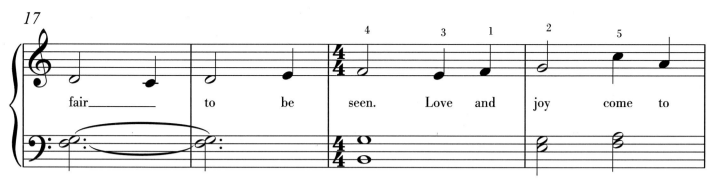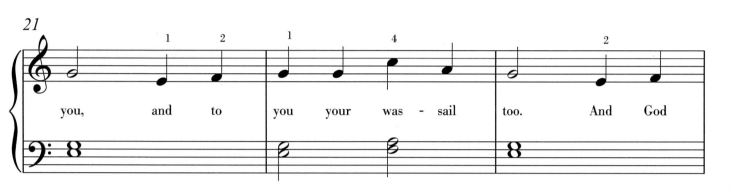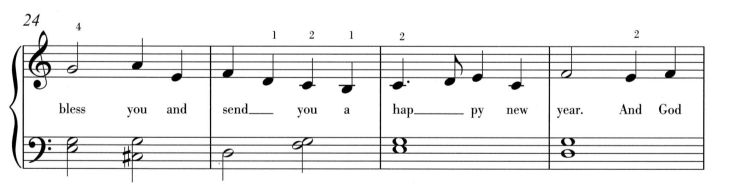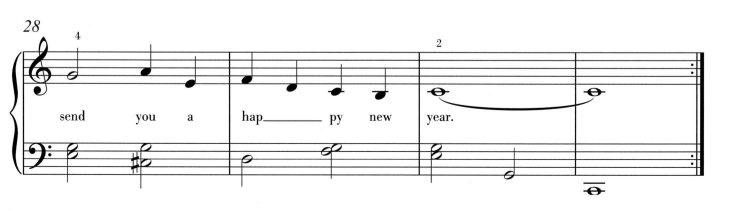

5. Jingle Bells

James Pierpont
Arr. Jennifer Eklund

Joyfully

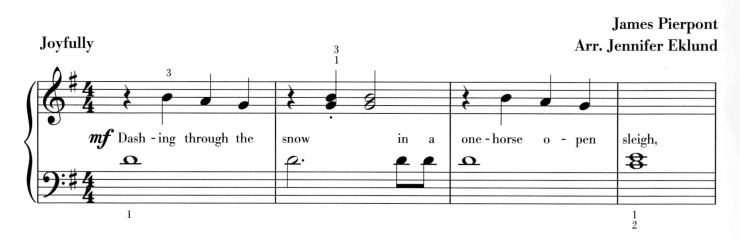
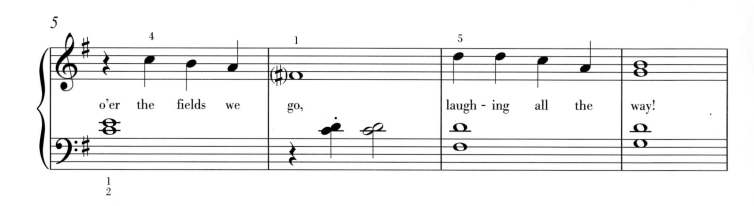
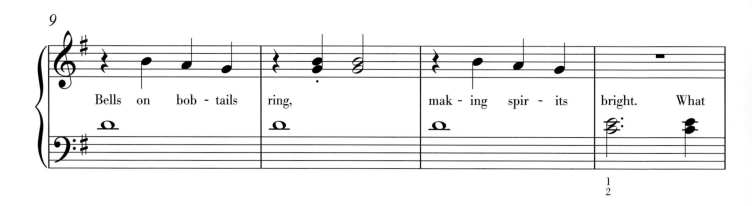
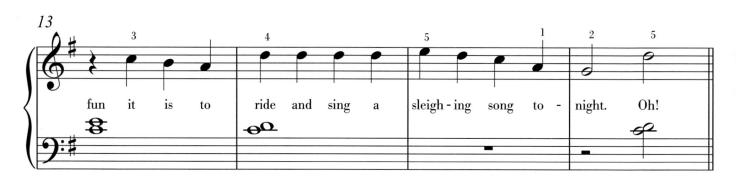

Copyright © 2015 Piano Pronto Publishing, Inc. (ASCAP)
All Rights Reserved | PianoPronto.com

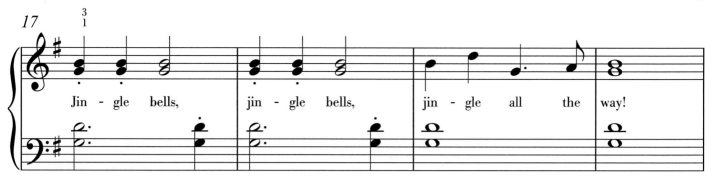

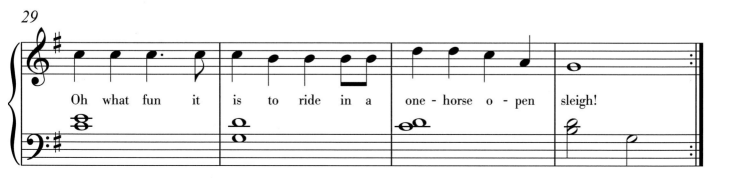

6. Joy to the World

George Frideric Handel
Arr. Jennifer Eklund

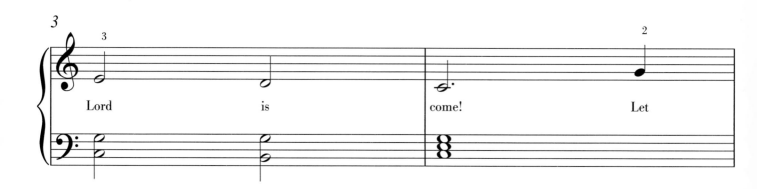
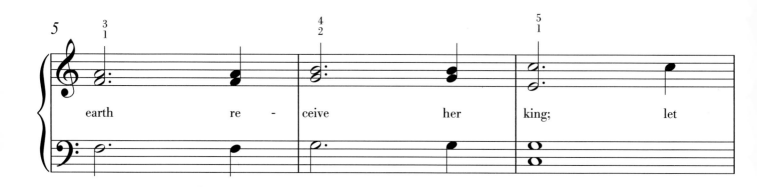
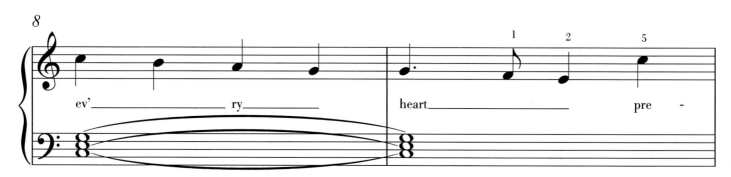

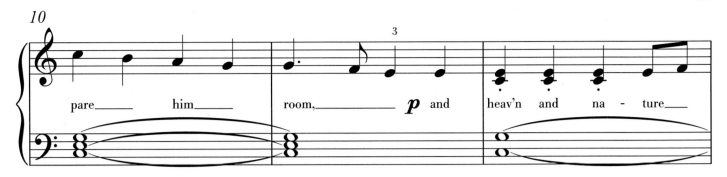
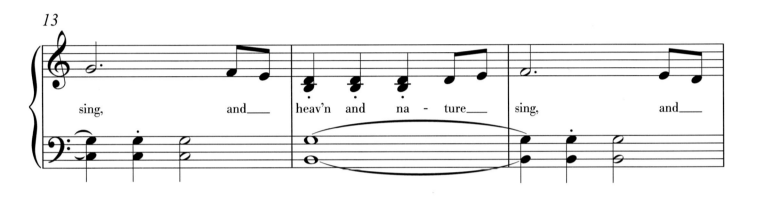
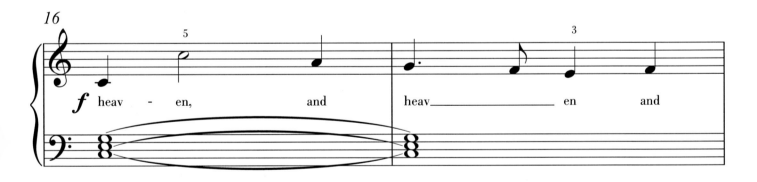
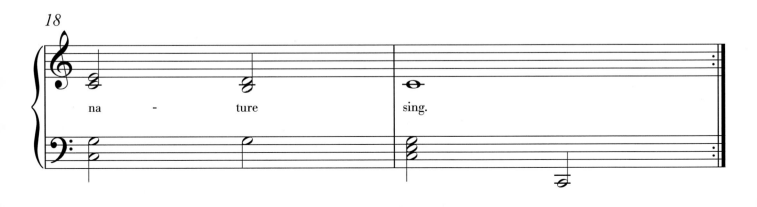

7. Silent Night

Franz Gruber
Arr. Jennifer Eklund

Peacefully

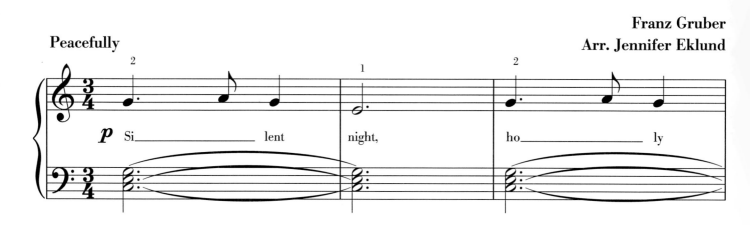
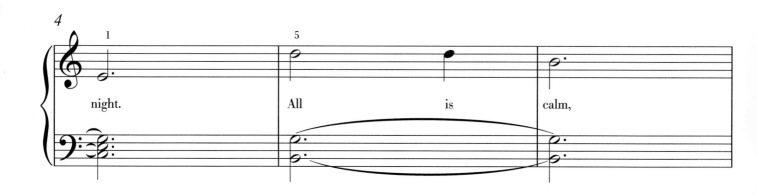
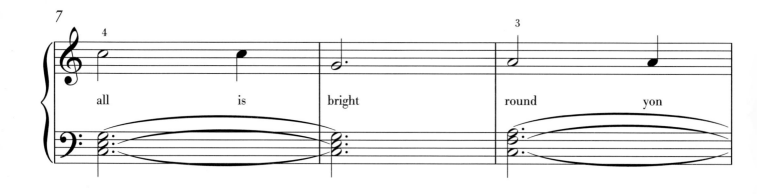
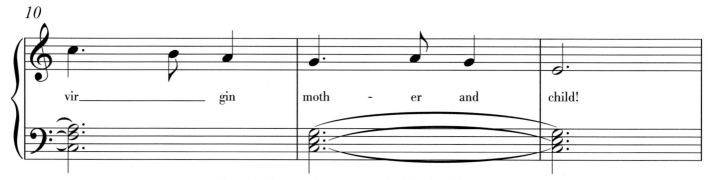

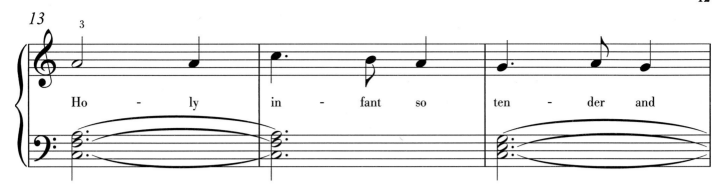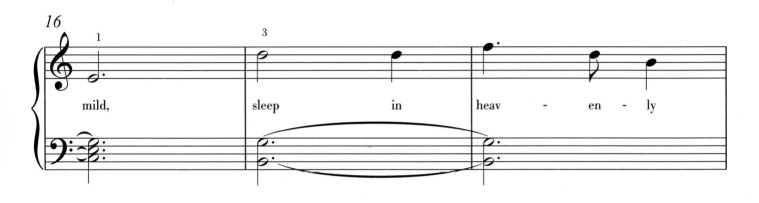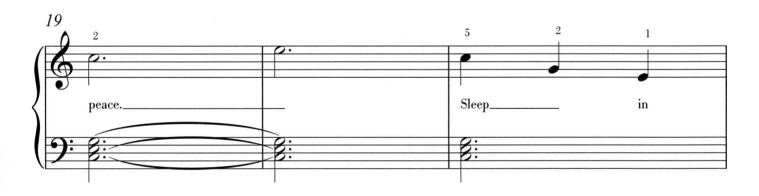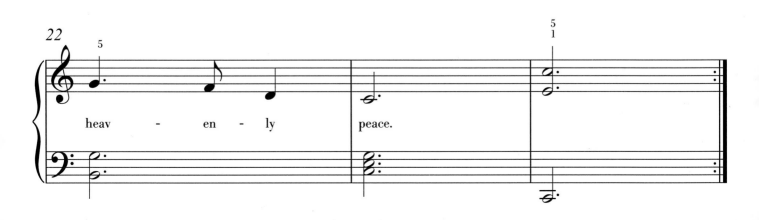

8. The First Noel

Traditional
Arr. Jennifer Eklund

Moderately

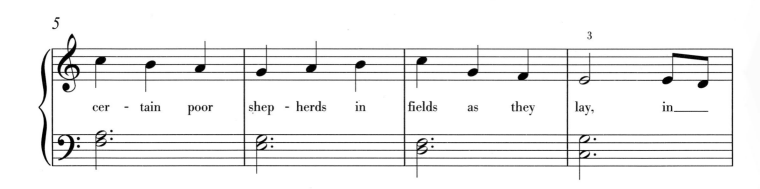

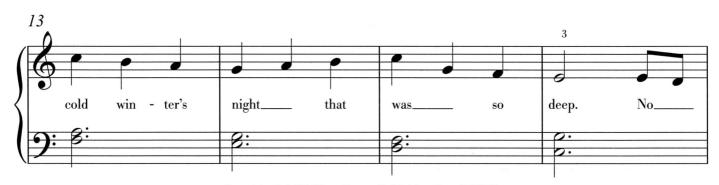

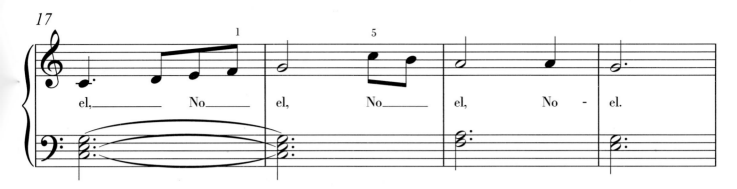

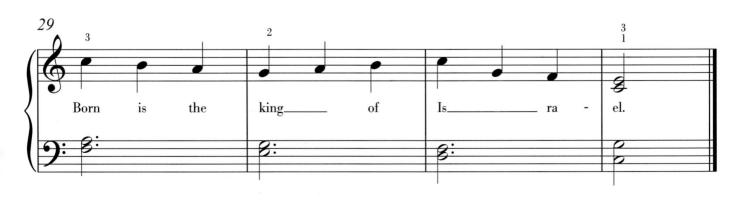

9. We Three Kings

John H. Hopkins
Arr. Jennifer Eklund

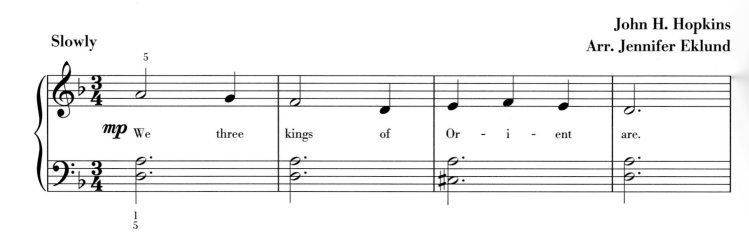
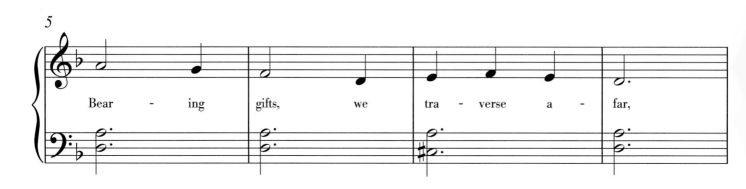
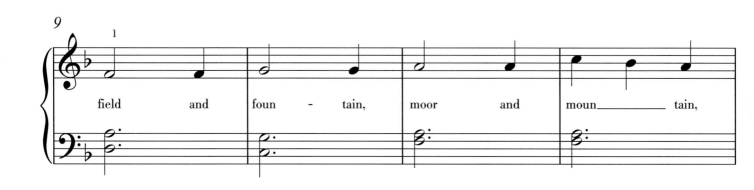

Copyright © 2015 Piano Pronto Publishing, Inc. (ASCAP)
All Rights Reserved | PianoPronto.com

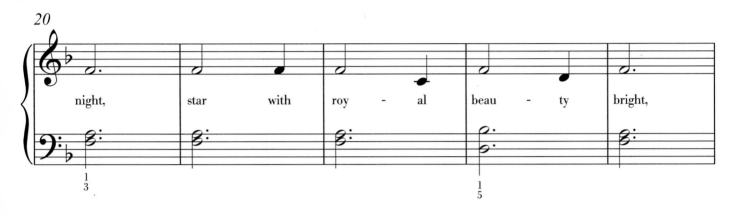
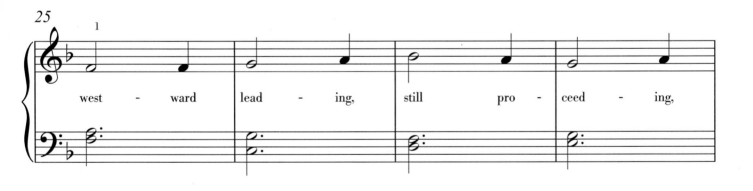
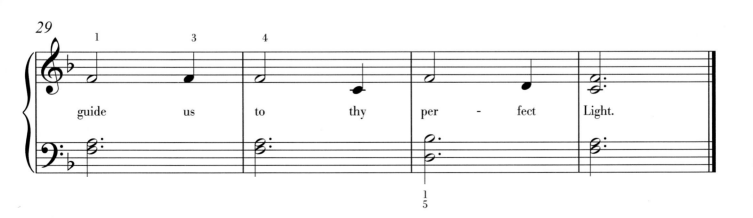

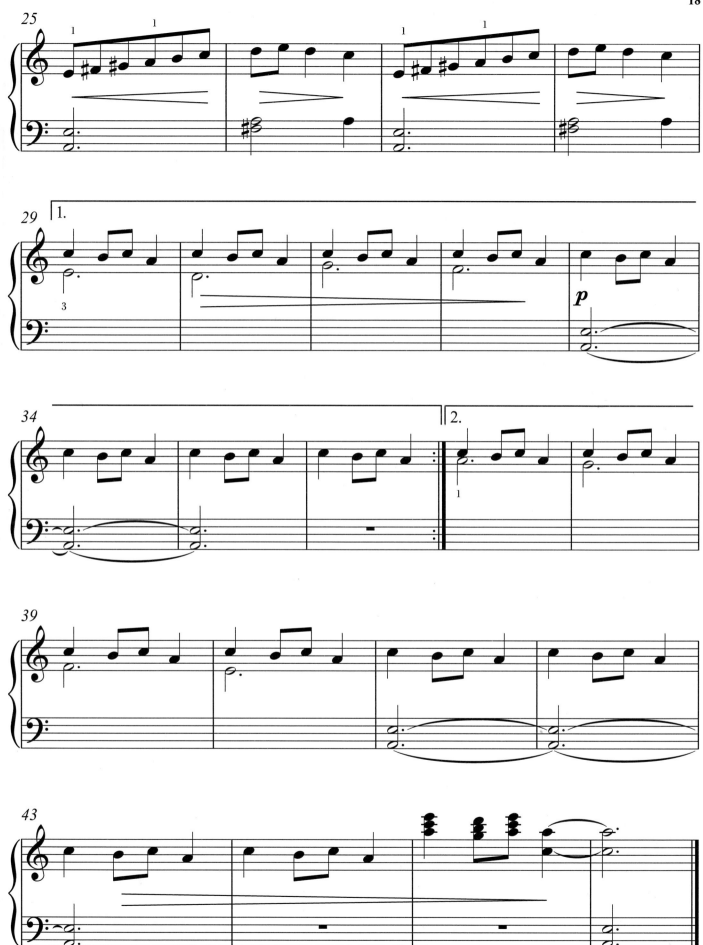

11. We Wish You a Merry Christmas

Traditional
Arr. Jennifer Eklund

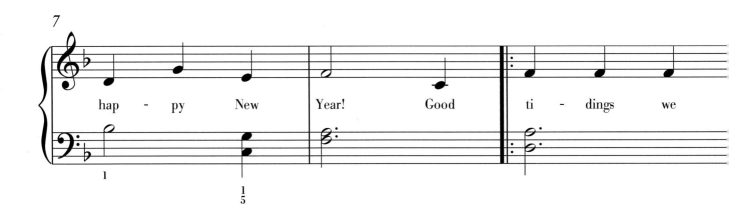
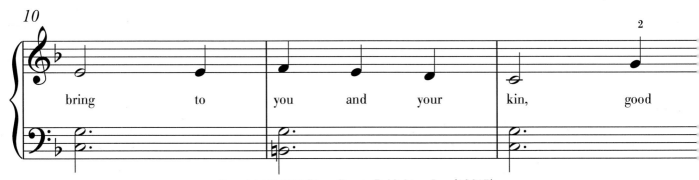

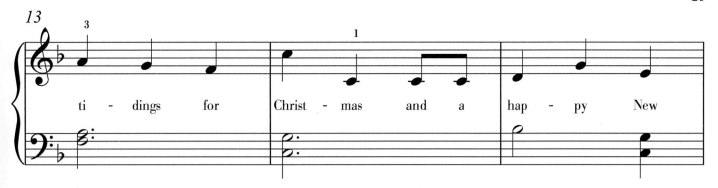

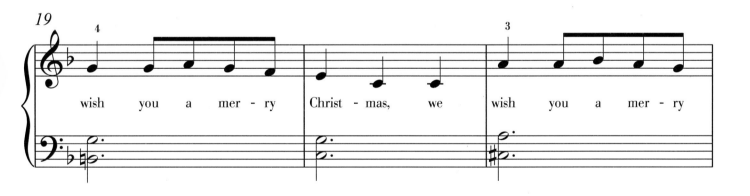
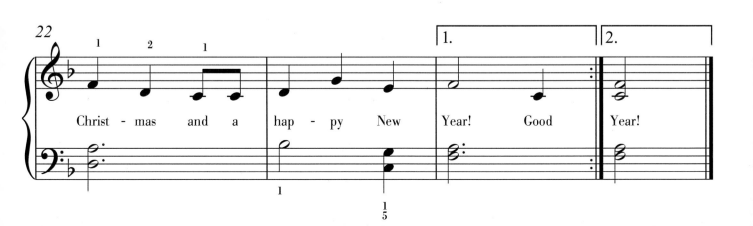

12. O Holy Night

Adolphe Adam
Arr. Jennifer Eklund

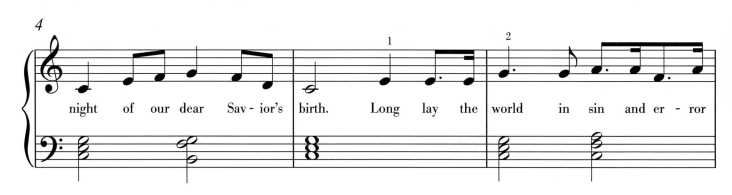
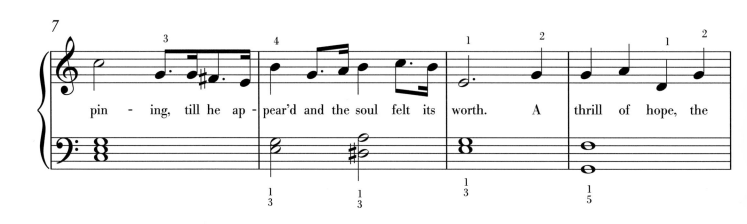
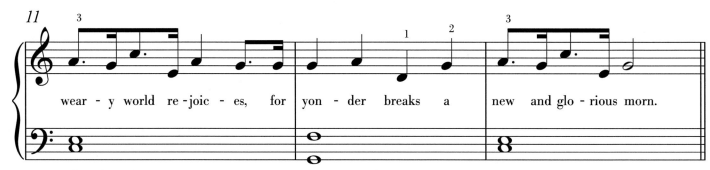

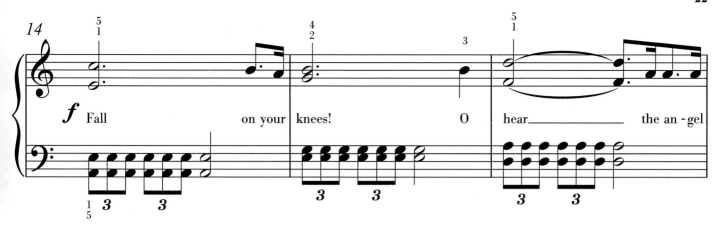
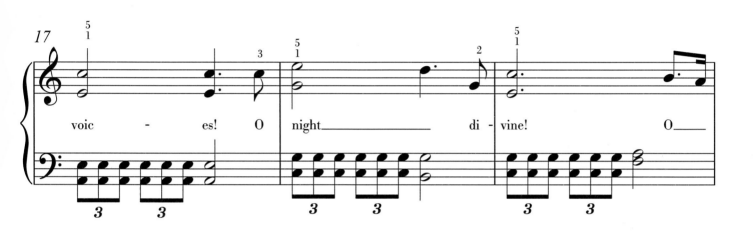
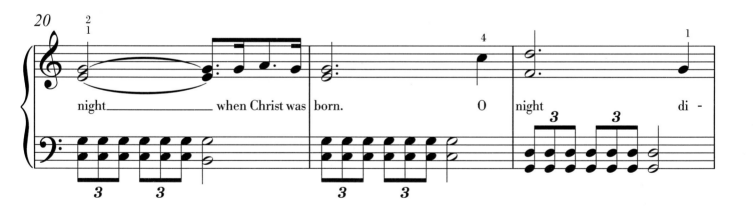
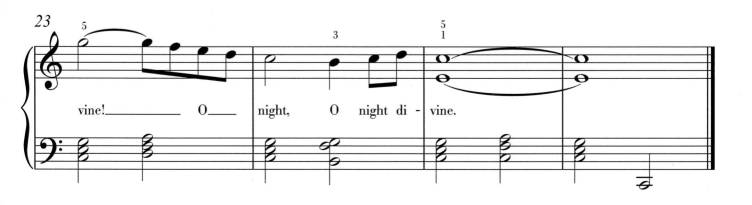

14. The Twelve Days of Christmas

Traditional
Arr. Jennifer Eklund

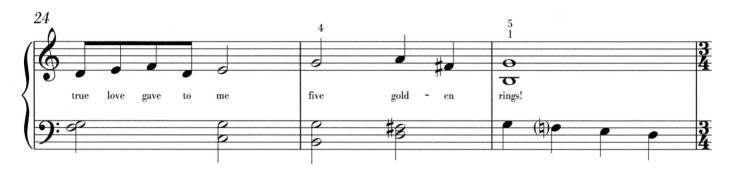

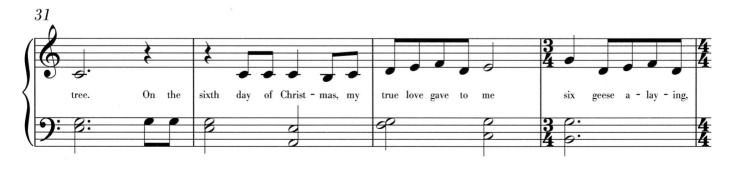

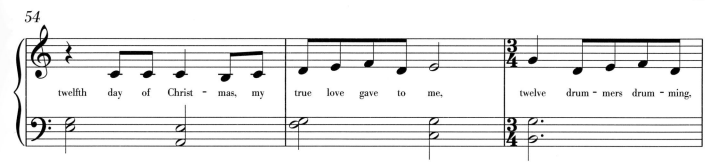
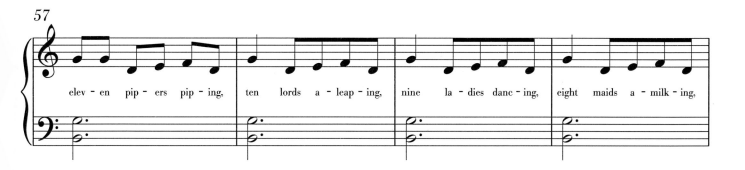
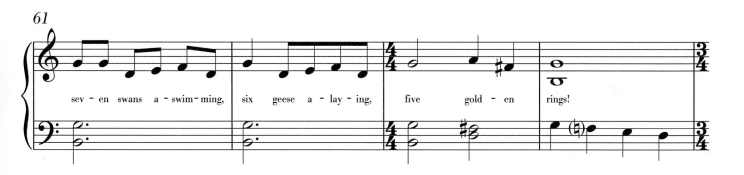
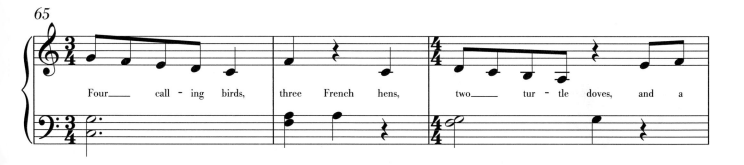
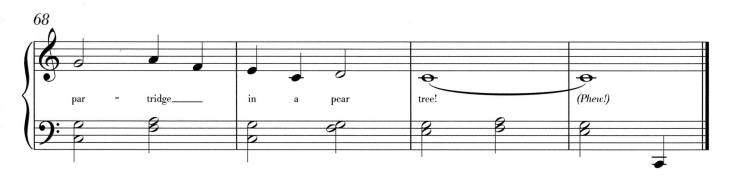

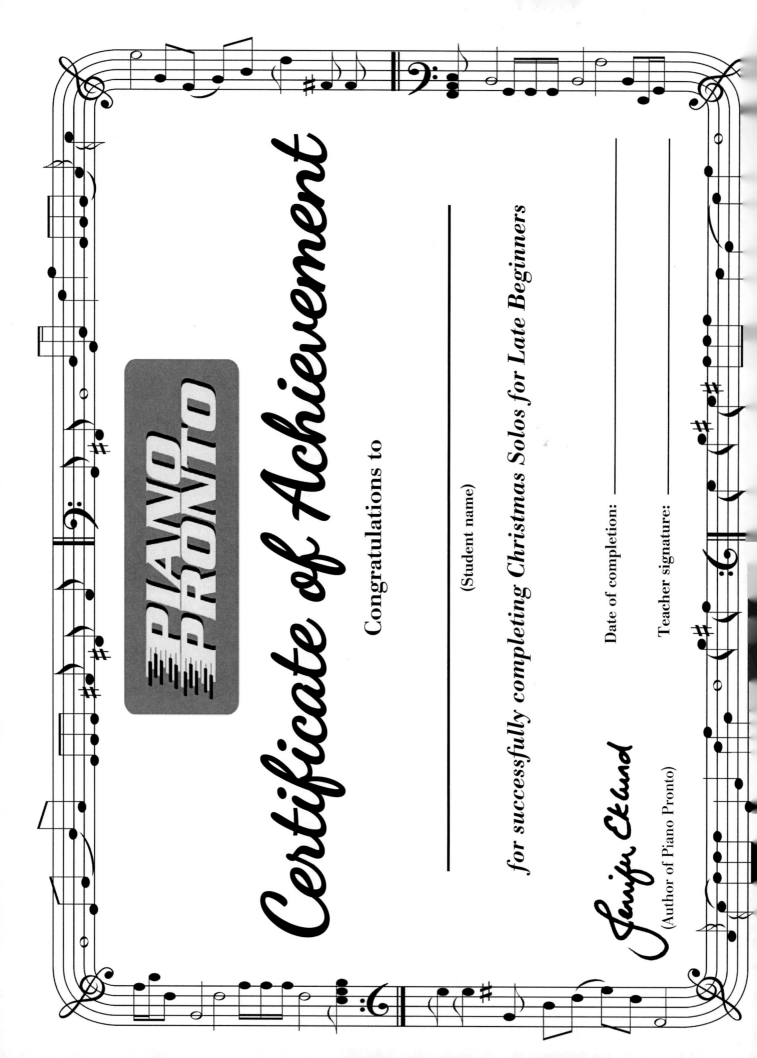